Who can resist making dainty dresses for little girls? Here are four irresistible styles for size 12 to 18 months.



LEISURE ARTS, INC. • Maumelle, Arkansas

# Jasmine

EASY +

**Size:** 12 to 18 months

## SHOPPING LIST

### Yarn (Light Weight) LIGHT 3

[3 ounces, 330 yards
(85 grams, 301 meters) per skein]:

☐ 2 skeins

### Crochet Hook

☐ Size G (4 mm)
**or** size needed for gauge

### Additional Supplies

☐ Tapestry needle

## GAUGE INFORMATION

In Bodice pattern,
(sc, ch 1) 9 times and
21 rows/rnds = 4" (10 cm)
In Skirt pattern,
(sc, ch 2, 2 dc) 6 times and
11 rnds = 4" (10 cm)
**Gauge Swatch:** 4¼" x 4"
(10.75 cm x 10 cm)
Ch 20.
**Row 1:** Sc in second ch from hook, ★ ch 1, skip next ch, sc in next ch; repeat from ★ across: 10 sc and 9 ch-1 sps.
**Rows 2-21:** Ch 1, turn; sc in first sc, ★ ch 1, skip next ch-1 sp, sc in next sc; repeat from ★ across. Finish off.

## BODICE

Ch 84 loosely; being careful **not** to twist ch, join with slip st to form a ring.

**Rnd 1** (Right side)**:** Ch 1, sc in same st as joining, ch 1, skip next ch, ★ sc in next ch, ch 1, skip next ch; repeat from ★ around; join with slip st to first sc: 42 sc and 42 ch-1 sps.

***Note:*** Loop a short piece of yarn around any stitch to mark Rnd 1 as **right** side.

**Rnd 2:** Ch 1, turn; sc in same st as joining, ch 1, skip next ch-1 sp, ★ sc in next sc, ch 1, skip next ch-1 sp; repeat from ★ around; join with slip st to first sc.

Repeat Rnd 2 for pattern until Bodice measures approximately 3½" (9 cm) from beginning ch, ending by working a **wrong** side rnd.

## FIRST STRAP

**Row 1:** Turn; slip st in next 5 sts, ch 1, sc in next sc, ★ ch 1, skip next ch-1 sp, sc in next sc; repeat from ★ 2 times **more**, leave remaining sts unworked: 4 sc and 3 ch-1 sps.

**Row 2:** Ch 1, turn; sc in first sc, ★ ch 1, skip next ch-1 sp, sc in next sc; repeat from ★ 2 times **more**.

Repeat Row 2 until Strap measures approximately 4" (10 cm), ending by working a **wrong** side row.

Finish off.

## SECOND STRAP

**Row 1:** With **right** side facing, skip next 8 sc from First Strap and join yarn with sc in next sc ***(see Joining With Sc, page 22)***; ★ ch 1, skip next ch-1 sp, sc in next sc; repeat from ★ 2 times **more**, leave remaining sts unworked: 4 sc and 3 ch-1 sps.

Complete same as First Strap.

## THIRD STRAP

**Row 1:** With **right** side facing, skip next 5 sc from Second Strap and join yarn with sc in next sc; ★ ch 1, skip next ch-1 sp, sc in next sc; repeat from ★ 2 times **more**, leave remaining sts unworked: 4 sc and 3 ch-1 sps.

Complete same as First Strap, leaving a long end for sewing.

## FOURTH STRAP

**Row 1:** With **right** side facing, skip next 8 sc from First Strap and join yarn with sc in next sc; ★ ch 1, skip next ch-1 sp, sc in next sc; repeat from ★ 2 times **more**, leave remaining 5 sts unworked: 4 sc and 3 ch-1 sps.

Complete same as First Strap, leaving a long end for sewing.

With **wrong** sides together and Bodice joining at side, using long ends and working through **both** loops of sts on **both** pieces, whipstitch shoulder seams ***(Fig. 7, page 23)***.

## SKIRT

**Rnd 1** (Eyelet rnd)**:** With **right** side of Bodice facing and working in free loops of beginning ch ***(Fig. 5b, page 23)***, join yarn with dc in same st as joining ***(see Joining With Dc, page 22)***; ch 1, skip next ch, ★ dc in next ch, ch 1, skip next ch; repeat from ★ around; join with slip st to first dc: 42 dc and 42 ch-1 sps.

**Rnd 2:** Ch 1, (sc, ch 2, 2 dc) in same st as joining, skip next ch-1 sp, ★ (sc, ch 2, 2 dc) in next dc, skip next ch-1 sp; repeat from ★ around; join with slip st to first sc: 84 dc, 42 sc, and 42 ch-2 sps.

**Rnd 3:** Slip st in next ch-2 sp, ch 1, turn; (sc, ch 2, 2 dc) in same sp, (sc, ch 2, 2 dc) in next ch-2 sp and in each ch-2 sp around; join with slip st to first sc.

Repeat Rnd 3 for pattern until Skirt measures approximately 8½" (21.5 cm), ending by working a **right** side rnd.

Finish off.

## TIE

Work a 50" (127 cm) long chain.

**Row 1:** Sc in back ridge of second ch from hook and each ch across ***(Fig. 3, page 22)***; finish off.

Beginning at center front, weave Tie through Eyelet rnd of Skirt.

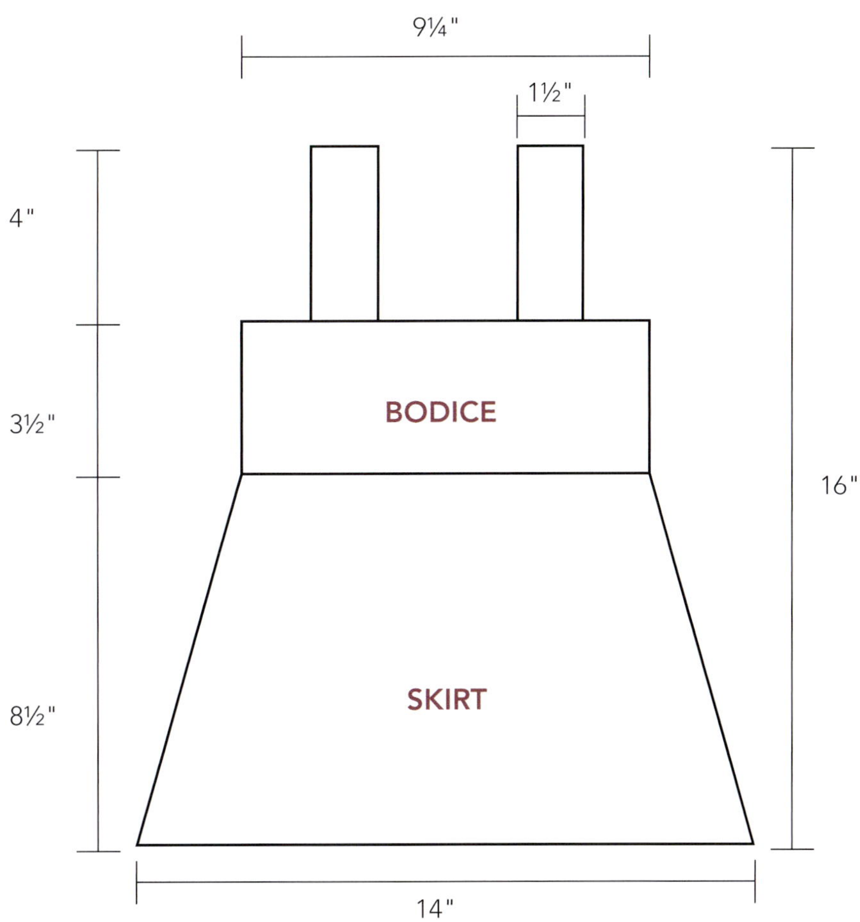

# Lexxi

EASY +

**Size:** 12 to 18 months

## SHOPPING LIST

### Yarn (Light Weight) LIGHT 3

[1.75 ounces, 136 yards
(50 grams, 125 meters) per skein]:

- ☐ Black - 3 skeins
- ☐ White - 1 skein
- ☐ Red - 10 yards (9 meters)

### Crochet Hook

- ☐ Size G (4 mm)
  **or** size needed for gauge

### Additional Supplies

- ☐ Tapestry needle

## GAUGE INFORMATION

In Body pattern,
(sc, dc) 9 times and
16 rows/rnds = 4" (10 cm)
In Skirt pattern,
3 repeats (15 sts and 3 ch-2 sps)
and 8 rnds = 3¼" (8.25 cm)

**Gauge Swatch:** 4" (10 cm) square
With Black, ch 19.
**Row 1** (Right side)**:** Sc in second ch from hook, dc in next ch, (sc in next ch, dc in next ch) across: 18 sts.
**Rows 2-16:** Ch 1, turn; sc in first dc, dc in next sc, (sc in next dc, dc in next sc) across.
Finish off.

## STITCH GUIDE

**TREBLE CROCHET *(abbreviated tr)***
YO twice, insert hook in sc indicated, YO and pull up a loop (4 loops on hook), (YO and draw through 2 loops on hook) 3 times.

**SINGLE CROCHET 2 TOGETHER *(abbreviated sc2tog)***
Pull up a loop in each of next 2 sts, YO and draw through all 3 loops on hook **(counts as one sc)**.

**DOUBLE CROCHET 2 TOGETHER *(abbreviated dc2tog)*** (uses next 2 sts)
★ YO, insert hook in **next** st, YO and pull up a loop, YO and draw through 2 loops on hook; repeat from ★ once **more**, YO and draw through all 3 loops on hook **(counts as one dc)**.

## BODY

With Black, ch 84 loosely; being careful **not** to twist ch, join with slip st to form a ring.

**Rnd 1** (Right side)**:** Ch 1, sc in same st as joining, dc in next ch, (sc in next ch, dc in next ch) around; join with slip st to first sc: 84 sts.

***Note:*** Loop a short piece of yarn around any stitch to mark Rnd 1 as **right** side.

**Rnd 2:** Ch 3 **(counts as first dc, now and throughout)**, turn; sc in next dc, (dc in next sc, sc in next dc) around; join with slip st to first dc.

**Rnd 3:** Ch 1, turn; sc in same st as joining, dc in next sc, (sc in next dc, dc in next sc) around; join with slip st to first sc.

Repeat Rnds 2 and 3 for pattern until Body measures approximately 7½" (19 cm) from beginning ch, ending by working Rnd 2.

## FRONT

### ARMHOLE SHAPING

**Row 1:** Turn; slip st in next 2 sts, [ch 2, dc in next sc **(counts as first dc2tog, now and throughout)**], (sc in next dc, dc in next sc) 17 times, sc2tog, leave remaining 44 sts unworked: 36 sts.

**Row 2:** Ch 1, turn; beginning in first sc, sc2tog, (dc in next sc, sc in next dc) across to last 2 sts, dc2tog: 34 sts.

**Row 3:** Ch 2, turn; dc in next sc, (sc in next dc, dc in next sc) across to last 2 sts, sc2tog: 32 sts.

**Row 4:** Ch 3, turn; sc in next dc, (dc in next sc, sc in next dc) across.

Repeat Row 4 until Armholes measure approximately 1¾" (4.5 cm), ending by working a **wrong** side row.

### NECK SHAPING

#### First Side

**Row 1:** Ch 3, turn; (sc in next dc, dc in next sc) 5 times, sc2tog, leave remaining 19 sts unworked: 12 sts.

**Row 2:** Ch 1, turn; beginning in first sc, sc2tog, (dc in next sc, sc in next dc) across: 11 sts.

**Row 3:** Ch 3, turn; (sc in next dc, dc in next sc) across to last 2 sts, sc2tog: 10 sts.

**Row 4:** Ch 1, turn; beginning in first sc, sc2tog, (dc in next sc, sc in next dc) across: 9 sts.

**Row 5:** Ch 3, turn; (sc in next dc, dc in next sc) across.

**Row 6:** Ch 1, turn; sc in first dc, (dc in next sc, sc in next dc) across.

Repeat Rows 5 and 6 until Armholes measure approximately 4" (10 cm), ending by working a **wrong** side row.

Finish off.

**Second Side**

**Row 1:** With **right** side facing, skip next 6 sts from First Side and join Black with slip st in next dc; ch 2, (dc in next sc, sc in next dc) across: 12 sts.

**Row 2:** Ch 3, turn; sc in next dc, (dc in next sc, sc in next dc) across to last 2 sts, dc2tog: 11 sts.

**Row 3:** Ch 2, turn; (dc in next sc, sc in next dc) across: 10 sts.

**Row 4:** Ch 3, turn; sc in next dc, (dc in next sc, sc in next dc) across to last 2 sts, dc2tog: 9 sts.

**Row 5:** Ch 1, turn; sc in first dc, (dc in next sc, sc in next dc) across.

**Row 6:** Ch 3, turn; (sc in next dc, dc in next sc) across.

Repeat Rows 5 and 6 until Armholes measure approximately 4" (10 cm), ending by working a **wrong** side row.

Finish off.

## BACK

### ARMHOLE SHAPING

**Row 1:** With **right** side facing, skip next 4 sts from Front and join Black with slip st in next dc; ch 2, dc in next sc, (sc in next dc, dc in next sc) 17 times, sc2tog, leave remaining sts unworked: 36 sts.

Complete same as Front, leaving long ends for sewing.

With **wrong** sides together and using long ends, working through **both** loops of sts on **both** pieces, whipstitch shoulder seams ***(Fig. 7, page 23)***.

### ARMHOLE TRIM

With **right** side facing, join Black with sc in third unworked st at either armhole; sc evenly around; join with slip st to first sc, finish off.

Repeat for second Armhole.

### NECK TRIM

With **right** side facing, join Black with sc in sc at center Back; sc evenly around; join with slip st to first sc, finish off.

## SKIRT

**Rnd 1:** With **right** side facing and working in free loops of beginning ch ***(Fig. 5b, page 23)***, join White with sc in same st as joining ***(see Joining With Sc, page 22)***; sc in each ch around; join with slip st to first sc: 84 sc.

**Rnds 2-9:** Ch 1, turn; sc in same st as joining and in each sc around; join with slip st to first sc.

**Rnd 10:** Ch 3, do **not** turn; dc in same st as joining, skip next sc, (dc, ch 2, dc) in next sc, skip next sc, ★ 3 dc in next sc, skip next sc, (dc, ch 2, dc) in next sc, skip next sc; repeat from ★ around, dc in same st as first dc; join with slip st to first dc: 105 dc and 21 ch-2 sps.

**Rnds 11-17:** Ch 3, dc in same st as joining, skip next 2 dc, (dc, ch 2, dc) in next ch-2 sp, skip next 2 dc, ★ 3 dc in next dc, skip next 2 dc, (dc, ch 2, dc) in next ch-2 sp, skip next 2 dc; repeat from ★ around, dc in same st as first dc; join with slip st to first dc.

Finish off.

## FLOWER

**Rnd 1** (Right side)**:** With Red and leaving a long end for sewing, ch 2, 6 sc in second ch from hook; join with slip st to first sc.

**Rnd 2:** Ch 1, (sc, tr) in same st as joining and in each sc around; join with slip st to first sc: 12 sts.

**Rnd 3:** Ch 2, skip next tr, ★ slip st in next sc, ch 2, skip next tr; repeat from ★ around; join with slip st to joining slip st: 6 ch-2 sps.

**Rnd 4:** (Slip st, ch 1, sc, hdc, 3 dc, hdc, sc) in first ch-2 sp **(petal made)**, (sc, hdc, 3 dc, hdc, sc) in next ch-2 sp and in each ch-2 sp around; join with slip st to first sc: 6 petals.

**Rnd 5:** Slip st in each st around; join with slip st to joining slip st, finish off.

Using photo on page 6 as a guide for placement and long end, sew Flower to Dress.

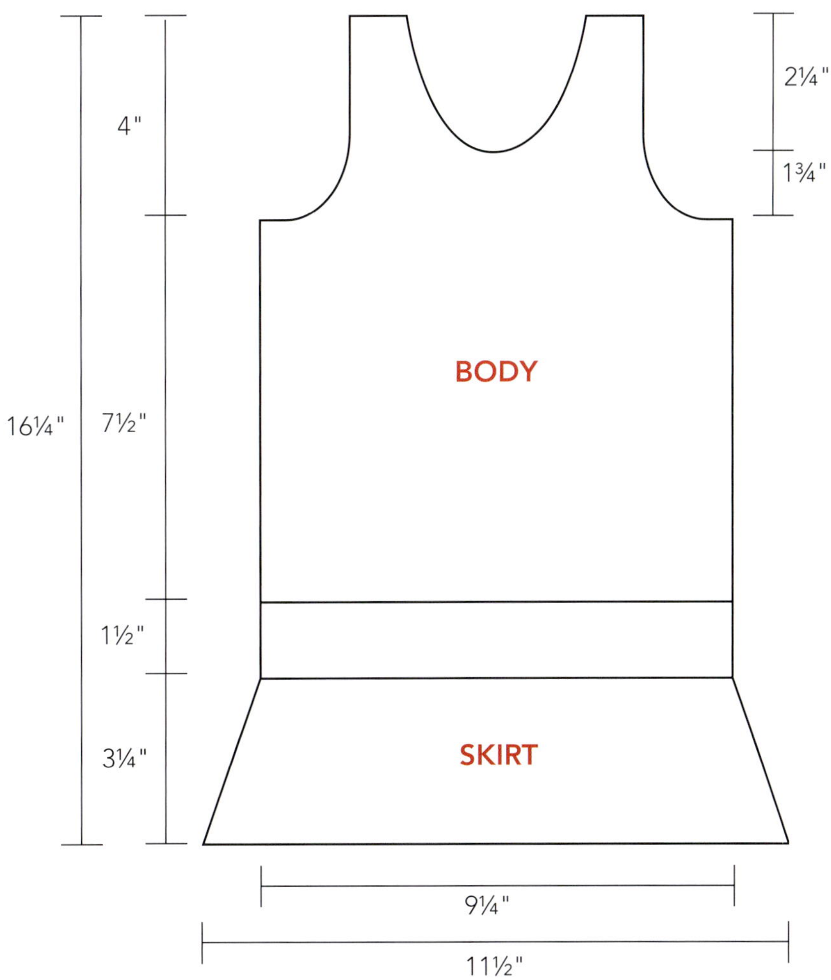

# Ashley

EASY +

**Size:** 12 to 18 months

## SHOPPING LIST

### Yarn (Light Weight) LIGHT 3

[5 ounces, 362 yards
(140 grams, 331 meters) per skein]:

- ☐ Tan - 1 skein
- ☐ Peach - 1 skein
- ☐ Variegated - 1 skein
- ☐ Rose - 40 yards (36.5 meters)
- ☐ White - 20 yards (18.5 meters)

### Crochet Hook

- ☐ Size G (4 mm)
  **or** size needed for gauge

## GAUGE INFORMATION

In Yoke pattern,
18 dc = 4" (10 cm)
Rnds 1-10 = 3¾" (9.5 cm)
In Skirt pattern,
(dc, ch 2, dc) 6 times and
8 rnds = 3" (7.5 cm)
**Gauge Swatch:** 4"(10 cm) square
Ch 20.
**Row 1:** Dc in fourth ch from hook **(3 skipped chs count as first dc)** and in each ch across: 18 dc.
**Rows 2-8:** Ch 3 **(counts as first dc)**, turn; dc in next dc and in each dc across.
Finish off.

## STITCH GUIDE

**TREBLE CROCHET *(abbreviated tr)***

YO twice, insert hook in sc indicated, YO and pull up a loop (4 loops on hook), (YO and draw through 2 loops on hook) 3 times.

**FOUNDATION DOUBLE CROCHET *(abbreviated Fdc)***

★ YO, insert hook in ch at base of Fdc just made ***(Fig. 2, page 22)***, YO and pull up a loop, YO and draw through one loop on hook **(ch made)**, (YO and draw through all 2 loops on hook) twice **(Fdc made)**; repeat from ★ for each additional Fdc.

**REVERSE SINGLE CROCHET *(abbreviated reverse sc)***

Working from **left** to **right**, insert hook in stitch to right of hook ***(Fig. A)***, YO and draw through, under and to left of loop on hook (2 loops on hook) ***(Fig. B)***, YO and draw through both loops on hook ***(Fig. C)*** **(reverse sc made, *Fig. D*)**.

**Fig. A**

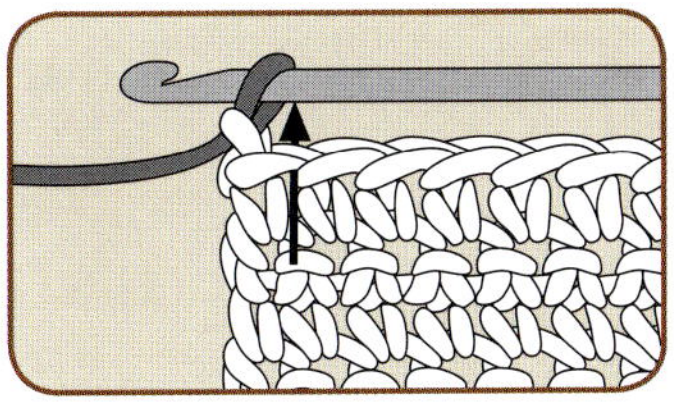

**Fig. B**

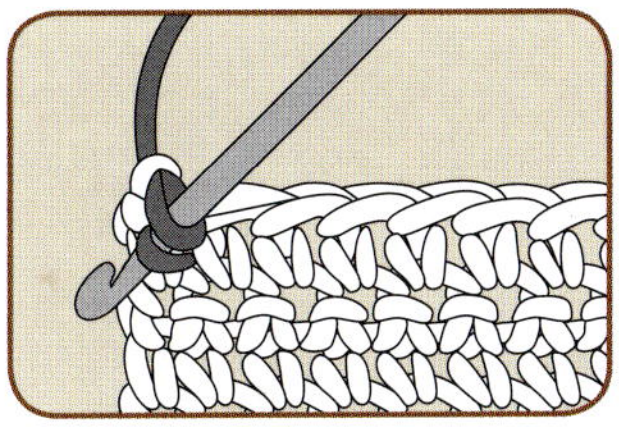

**Fig. C**

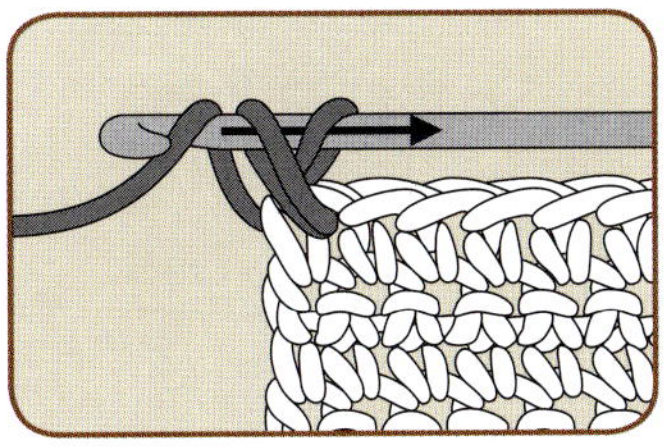

**Fig. D**

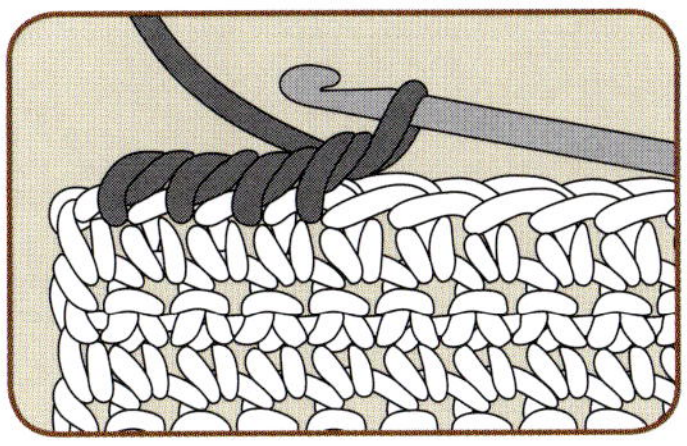

## YOKE

**Foundation Rnd:** With Tan, ch 4, YO, insert hook in fourth ch from hook **(3 skipped chs count as first Fdc)**, YO and pull up a loop (3 loops on hook), YO and draw through one loop on hook **(ch made)**, (YO and draw through 2 loops on hook) twice **(Fdc made)**, work Fdc for a total of 72 sts; join with slip st to first Fdc.

**Rnd 1** (Right side)**:** Ch 3, dc in next 2 Fdc, 2 dc in next Fdc, dc in next 4 Fdc, 2 dc in next Fdc, ★ dc in next 3 Fdc, 2 dc in next Fdc, dc in next 4 Fdc, 2 dc in next Fdc; repeat from ★ around; join with slip st to first dc: 88 dc.

***Note:*** Loop a short piece of yarn around any stitch to mark Rnd 1 as **right** side.

**Rnd 2:** Ch 1, sc in same st as joining, tr in next dc, (sc in next dc, tr in next dc) around; join with slip st to first sc.

**Rnd 3:** Ch 3, dc in next 3 sts, 2 dc in next sc, dc in next 5 sts, 2 dc in next sc, ★ dc in next 4 sts, 2 dc in next st, dc in next 5 sts, 2 dc in next st; repeat from ★ around; join with slip st to first dc: 104 dc.

**Rnd 4:** Ch 1, sc in same st as joining, tr in next dc, (sc in next dc, tr in next dc) around; join with slip st to first sc.

**Rnd 5:** Ch 3, dc in next 4 sts, 2 dc in next tr, dc in next 6 sts, 2 dc in next sc, ★ dc in next 5 sts, 2 dc in next st, dc in next 6 sts, 2 dc in next st; repeat from ★ around; join with slip st to first dc: 120 dc.

**Rnd 6:** Ch 1, sc in same st as joining, tr in next dc, (sc in next dc, tr in next dc) around; join with slip st to first sc.

**Rnd 7:** Ch 3, dc in next 5 sts, 2 dc in next st, dc in next 7 sts, 2 dc in next st, ★ dc in next 6 sts, 2 dc in next st, dc in next 7 sts, 2 dc in next st; repeat from ★ around; join with slip st to first dc: 136 dc.

**Rnd 8:** Ch 1, sc in same st as joining, tr in next dc, (sc in next dc, tr in next dc) around; join with slip st to first sc.

**Rnd 9:** Ch 3, dc in next 4 sts, 2 dc in next st, ★ (dc in next 6 sts, 2 dc in next st) 5 times, dc in next 5 sts, 2 dc in next st; repeat from ★ around to last 7 sts, dc in next 6 sts, 2 dc in last tr; join with slip st to first dc: 156 dc.

**Rnd 10:** Ch 1, sc in same st as joining, tr in next dc, (sc in next dc, tr in next dc) around; join with slip st to first sc; do **not** finish off.

## SKIRT

**Rnd 1:** Ch 3, dc in next 20 sts, ch 2, skip next 36 sts **(armhole)**, dc in next 42 sts, ch 2, skip next 36 sts **(armhole)**, dc in last 21 sts; join with slip st to first dc: 84 dc and 4 chs.

**Rnd 2:** Ch 2, turn; hdc in next 21 dc, hdc in next 2 chs, hdc in next 42 dc, hdc in next 2 chs, hdc in last 20 hdc; join with slip st to Back Loop Only of first hdc ***(Fig. 4, page 22)***: 88 hdc.

**Rnd 3:** Ch 2, turn; working from **left** to **right**, work reverse sc in Front Loop Only of each hdc around ***(Figs. A-D, page 18)***; join with slip st to first st.

**Rnd 4:** Ch 1, do **not** turn; working in free loops on Rnd 2 ***(Fig. 5a, page 23)***, (dc, ch 1, dc) in first hdc, skip next hdc, ★ (dc, ch 1, dc) in next hdc, skip next hdc; repeat from ★ around; join with slip st to first dc: 88 dc and 44 ch-1 sps.

**Rnds 5-7:** Slip st in first ch-1 sp, ch 4 **(counts as first dc plus ch 1, now and throughout)**, dc in same sp, (dc, ch 1, dc) in next ch-1 sp and in each ch-1 sp around; join with slip st to first dc.

Finish off.

**Rnd 8:** With **right** side facing, join Peach in first ch-1 sp ***(see Joining With Dc, page 22)***; ch 1, dc in same sp, (dc, ch 1, dc) in next ch-1 sp and in each ch-1 sp around; join with slip st to first dc.

**Rnds 9-15:** Slip st in first ch-1 sp, ch 4, dc in same sp, (dc, ch 1, dc) in next ch-1 sp and in each ch-1 sp around; join with slip st to first dc.

Finish off.

**Rnd 16:** With **right** side facing facing, join Variegated with dc in first ch-1 sp; ch 2, dc in same sp, (dc, ch 2, dc) in next ch-1 sp and in each ch-1 sp around; join with slip st to first dc: 88 dc and 44 ch-2 sps.

**Rnds 17-22:** Slip st in first ch-2 sp, ch 5 **(counts as first dc plus ch 2)**, dc in same sp, (dc, ch 2, dc) in next ch-2 sp and in each ch-2 sp around; join with slip st to first dc.

Finish off.

**Rnd 23:** With **right** side facing, join Rose with dc in first ch-2 sp; ch 3, dc in same sp, (dc, ch 3, dc) in next ch-2 sp and in each ch-2 sp around; join with slip st to first dc: 44 ch-3 sps.

**Rnd 24:** (Slip st, 5 sc) in first ch-3 sp, 5 sc in next ch-3 sp and in each ch-3 sp around; join with slip st to first sc, finish off.

**Rnd 25:** With **right** side facing, working **behind** Rnd 24 ***(Fig. 6, page 23)*** and in skipped dc on Rnd 23, join White with dc in last dc; ch 3, dc in third ch from hook, dc in next dc, ★ dc in next dc, ch 3, dc in third ch from hook, dc in next dc; repeat from ★ around; join with slip st to first dc, finish off.

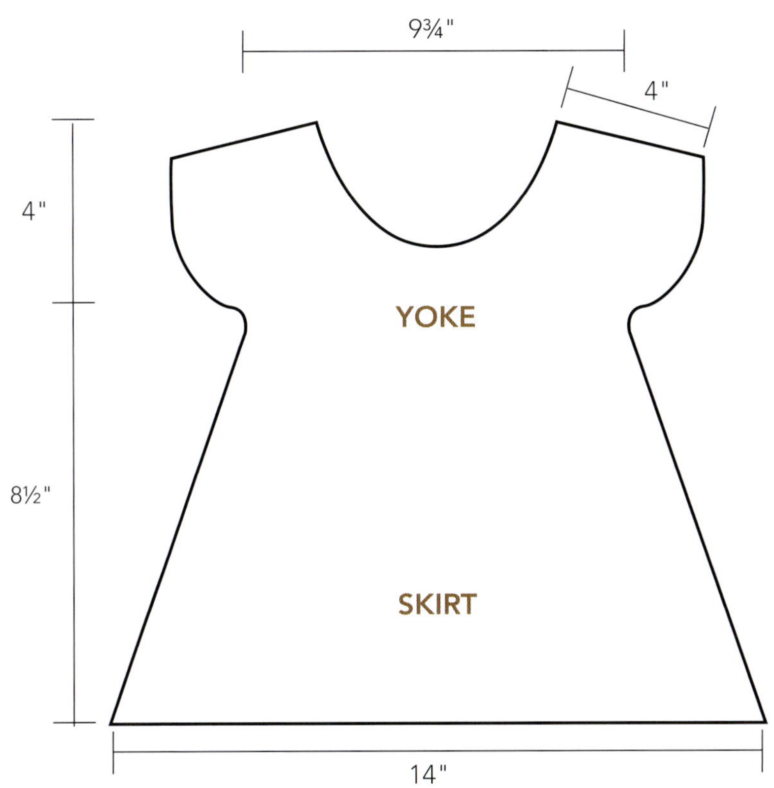

# Kate

EASY +

**Size:** 12 to 18 months

## SHOPPING LIST

### Yarn (Light Weight) LIGHT 3

[5 ounces, 362 yards
(140 grams, 331 meters) per skein]:

☐ Aqua - 1 skein

[3.5 ounces, 394 yards
(100 grams, 360 meters) per skein]:

☐ Variegated - 1 skein

### Crochet Hook

☐ Size G (4 mm)
**or** size needed for gauge

## GAUGE INFORMATION

In Yoke pattern,
18 sts and 15 rows/rnds = 4" (10 cm)
In Skirt pattern,
2 repeats (14 dc and 2 ch-2 sps)
and 7 rnds = 3¼" (8.25 cm)

**Gauge Swatch:** 4" (10 cm) square

With Aqua, ch 19.

**Row 1:** Hdc in third ch from hook and in each ch across: 18 hdc.

**Row 2:** Ch 1, turn; sc in Back Loop Only of each hdc across ***(Fig. 4, page 22)***.

**Row 3:** Ch 2 **(counts as first hdc)**, turn; hdc in both loops of next sc and each sc across.

**Rows 4-15:** Repeat Rows 2 and 3, 6 times.

Finish off.

## STITCH GUIDE

### FOUNDATION HALF DOUBLE CROCHET *(abbreviated Fhdc)*

★ YO, insert hook in ch at base of Fhdc just made ***(Fig. 1, page 22)***, YO and pull up a loop, YO and draw through one loop on hook **(ch made)**, YO and draw through all 3 loops on hook **(Fhdc made)**; repeat from ★ for each additional Fhdc.

## YOKE

**Foundation Rnd:** With Aqua, ch 3, YO, insert hook in third ch from hook **(2 skipped chs count as first Fhdc)**, YO and pull up a loop (3 loops on hook), YO and draw through one loop on hook **(ch made)**, YO and draw through all 3 loops on hook **(Fhdc made)**, work Fhdc for a total of 72 sts; join with slip st to Front Loop Only of first Fhdc ***(Fig. 4, page 22)***.

**Rnd 1** (Right side)**:** Ch 1, turn; working in Back Loops Only ***(Fig. 4, page 22)***, sc in same st as joining and in next 10 Fhdc, 2 sc in next Fhdc, (sc in next 11 Fhdc, 2 sc in next Fhdc) around; join with slip st to **both** loops of first sc: 78 sc.

***Note:*** Loop a short piece of yarn around any stitch to mark Rnd 1 as **right** side.

**Rnd 2:** Ch 2 **(counts as first hdc, now and throughout)**, turn; working in both loops, hdc in next 4 sc, 2 hdc in next sc, (hdc in next 12 sc, 2 hdc in next sc) around to last 7 sc, hdc in last 7 sc; join with slip st to Front Loop Only of first hdc: 84 hdc.

**Rnd 3:** Ch 1, turn; working in Back Loops Only, sc in same st as joining and in next 12 hdc, 2 sc in next hdc, (sc in next 13 hdc, 2 sc in next hdc) around; join with slip st to **both** loops of first sc: 90 sc.

**Rnd 4:** Ch 2, turn; working in both loops, hdc in next 6 sc, 2 hdc in next sc, (hdc in next 14 sc, 2 hdc in next sc) around to last 7 sc, hdc in last 7 sc; join with slip st to Front Loop Only of first hdc: 96 hdc.

**Rnd 5:** Ch 1, turn; working in Back Loops Only, sc in same st as joining and in next 14 hdc, 2 sc in next hdc, (sc in next 15 hdc, 2 sc in next hdc) around; join with slip st to **both** loops of first sc: 102 sc.

**Rnd 6:** Ch 2, turn; working in both loops, hdc in next 8 sc, 2 hdc in next sc, (hdc in next 16 sc, 2 hdc in next sc) around to last 7 sc, hdc in last 7 sc; join with slip st to Front Loop Only of first hdc: 108 hdc.

**Rnd 7:** Ch 1, turn; working in Back Loops Only, sc in same st as joining and in next 16 hdc, 2 sc in next hdc, (sc in next 17 hdc, 2 sc in next hdc) around; join with slip st to **both** loops of first sc: 114 sc.

**Rnd 8:** Ch 2, turn; working in both loops, hdc in next 10 sc, 2 hdc in next sc, (hdc in next 18 sc, 2 hdc in next sc) around to last 7 sc, hdc in last 7 sc; join with slip st to Front Loop Only of first hdc: 120 hdc.

**Rnd 9:** Ch 1, turn; working in Back Loops Only, sc in same st as joining and in next 18 hdc, 2 sc in next hdc, (sc in next 19 hdc, 2 sc in next hdc) around; join with slip st to **both** loops of first sc: 126 sc.

**Rnd 10:** Ch 2, turn; working in both loops, hdc in next 12 sc, 2 hdc in next sc, (hdc in next 20 sc, 2 hdc in next sc) around to last 7 sc, hdc in last 7 sc; join with slip st to Front Loop Only of first hdc: 132 hdc.

**Rnd 11:** Ch 1, turn; working in Back Loops Only, sc in same st as joining and in next 20 hdc, 2 sc in next hdc, (sc in next 21 hdc, 2 sc in next hdc) around; join with slip st to **both** loops of first sc: 138 sc.

**Rnd 12:** Ch 2, turn; working in both loops, hdc in next 14 sc, 2 hdc in next sc, (hdc in next 22 sc, 2 hdc in next sc) around to last 7 sc, hdc in last 7 sc; join with slip st to Front Loop Only of first hdc: 144 hdc.

**Rnd 13:** Ch 1, turn; working in Back Loops Only, sc in same st as joining and in next 22 hdc, 2 sc in next hdc, (sc in next 23 hdc, 2 sc in next hdc) around; join with slip st to **both** loops of first sc: 150 sc.

**Rnd 14:** Ch 2, turn; working in both loops, hdc in next 16 sc, 2 hdc in next sc, (hdc in next 24 sc, 2 hdc in next sc) around to last 7 sc, hdc in last 7 sc; join with slip st to Front Loop Only of first hdc, finish off: 156 hdc.

## SKIRT

**Rnd 1:** With **right** side facing and working in Back Loops Only, join Variegated with sc in same st as joining ***(see Joining With Sc, page 22)***, sc in next 41 hdc, ch 2, skip next 36 hdc **(armhole)**, sc in next 42 hdc, ch 2, skip last 36 hdc **(armhole)**; join with slip st to **both** loops of first sc: 84 sc and 4 chs.

**Rnd 2:** Ch 2, turn; working in both loops, hdc in next 2 chs, hdc in next 42 sc, hdc in next 2 chs, hdc in last 41 sc; join with slip st to Back Loop Only of first hdc: 88 hdc.

**Rnd 3:** Ch 1, turn; working in Back Loops Only, sc in same st as joining and in each hdc around; join with slip st to **both** loops of first sc.

**Rnd 4:** Ch 2, turn; working in both loops, 2 hdc in next sc, hdc in next 43 sc, 2 hdc in next sc, 2 hdc in next sc, hdc in last 42 sc; join with slip st to first hdc: 90 hdc.

**Rnd 5:** Ch 3, turn; dc in next hdc, skip next hdc, (2 dc, ch 2, 2 dc) in next hdc, ★ skip next hdc, dc in next 3 hdc, skip next hdc, (2 dc, ch 2, 2 dc) in next hdc; repeat from ★ around to last 2 hdc, skip next hdc, dc in last hdc; join with slip st to first dc: 105 dc and 15 ch-2 sps.

**Rnd 6:** Ch 3, do **not** turn; dc in next dc, skip next 2 dc, (2 dc, ch 2, 2 dc) in next ch-2 sp, ★ skip next 2 dc, dc in next 3 dc, skip next 2 dc, (2 dc, ch 2, 2 dc) in next ch-2 sp; repeat from ★ around to last 3 dc, skip next 2 dc, dc in last dc; join with slip st to first dc.

**Rnds 7-21:** Ch 3, dc in next dc, skip next 2 dc, (2 dc, ch 2, 2 dc) in next ch-2 sp, ★ skip next 2 dc, dc in next 3 dc, skip next 2 dc, (2 dc, ch 2, 2 dc) in next ch-2 sp; repeat from ★ around to last 3 dc, skip next 2 dc, dc in last dc; join with slip st to first dc.

Finish off.

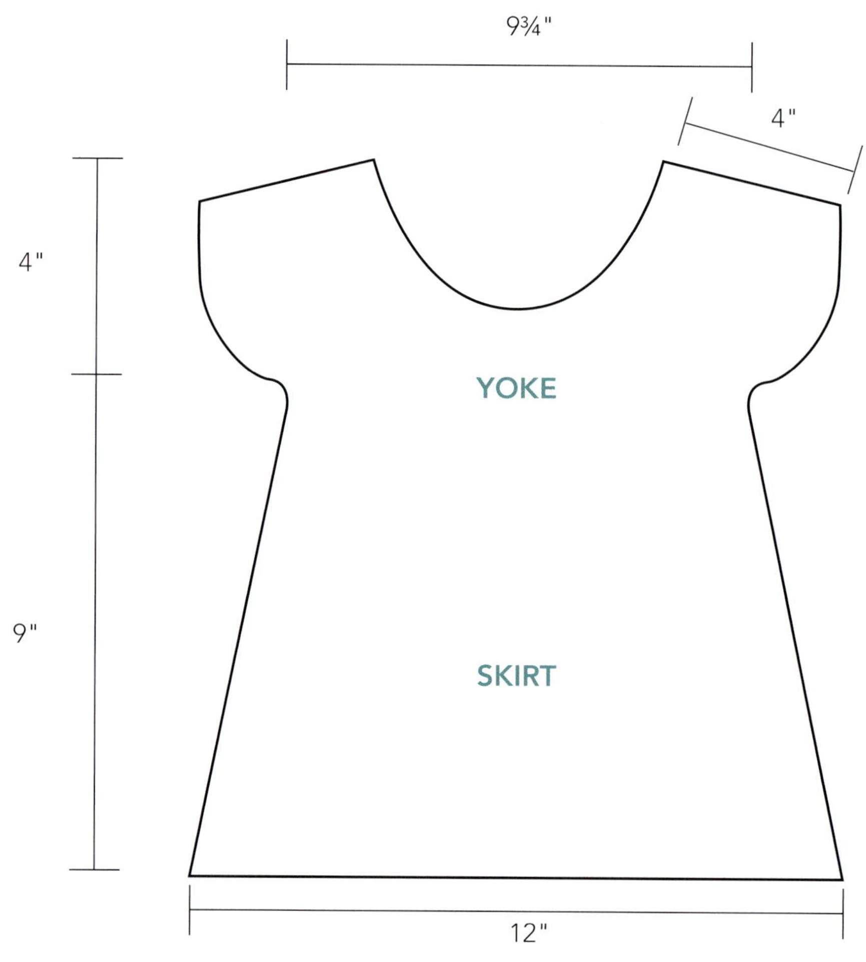

# GENERAL INSTRUCTIONS

## ABBREVIATIONS

| | |
|---|---|
| ch(s) | chain(s) |
| cm | centimeters |
| dc | double crochet(s) |
| Fdc | Foundation double crochet(s) |
| Fhdc | Foundation half double crochet(s) |
| dc2tog | double crochet 2 together |
| hdc | half double crochet(s) |
| mm | millimeters |
| Rnd(s) | Round(s) |
| sc | single crochet(s) |
| sc2tog | single crochet 2 together |
| sp(s) | space(s) |
| st(s) | stitch(es) |
| tr | treble crochet(s) |
| YO | yarn over |

## SYMBOLS & TERMS

★ — work instructions following ★ as many **more** times as indicated in addition to the first time.

( ) or **[ ]** — work enclosed instructions **as many** times as specified by the number immediately following **or** work all enclosed instructions in the stitch or space indicated **or** contains explanatory remarks.

colon (:) — the number(s) given after a colon at the end of a row or round denote(s) the number of stitches or spaces you should have on that row or round.

## GAUGE

Exact gauge is **essential** for proper fit. Before beginning your project, make the sample swatch given in the individual instructions in the yarn and hook specified. After completing the swatch, measure it, counting your stitches and rows carefully. If your swatch is larger or smaller than specified, **make another, changing hook size to get the correct gauge**. Keep trying until you find the size hook that will give you the specified gauge.

| CROCHET TERMINOLOGY | | |
|---|---|---|
| UNITED STATES | | INTERNATIONAL |
| slip stitch (slip st) | = | single crochet (sc) |
| single crochet (sc) | = | double crochet (dc) |
| half double crochet (hdc) | = | half treble crochet (htr) |
| double crochet (dc) | = | treble crochet (tr) |
| treble crochet (tr) | = | double treble crochet (dtr) |
| double treble crochet (dtr) | = | triple treble crochet (ttr) |
| triple treble crochet (tr tr) | = | quadruple treble crochet (qtr) |
| skip | = | miss |

| | |
|---|---|
| BEGINNER | Projects for first-time crocheters using basic stitches. Minimal shaping. |
| EASY | Projects using yarn with basic stitches, repetitive stitch patterns, simple color changes, and simple shaping and finishing. |
| INTERMEDIATE | Projects using a variety of techniques, such as basic lace patterns or color patterns, mid-level shaping and finishing. |
| EXPERIENCED | Projects with intricate stitch patterns, techniques and dimension, such as non-repeating patterns, multi-color techniques, fine threads, small hooks, detailed shaping and refined finishing. |

| CROCHET HOOKS | | | | | | | | | | | | | | | | | |
|---|---|---|---|---|---|---|---|---|---|---|---|---|---|---|---|---|---|
| **U.S.** | B-1 | C-2 | D-3 | E-4 | F-5 | G-6 | 7 | H-8 | I-9 | J-10 | K-10½ | L-11 | M/N-13 | N/P-15 | P/Q | Q | S |
| **Metric - mm** | 2.25 | 2.75 | 3.25 | 3.5 | 3.75 | 4 | 4.5 | 5 | 5.5 | 6 | 6.5 | 8 | 9 | 10 | 15 | 16 | 19 |

## JOINING WITH SC

When instructed to join with sc, begin with a slip knot on hook. Insert hook in stitch or space indicated, YO and pull up a loop, YO and draw through both loops on hook.

## JOINING WITH DC

When instructed to join with dc, begin with a slip knot on hook. YO, holding loop on hook, insert hook in space indicated, YO and pull up a loop (3 loops on hook), (YO and draw through 2 loops on hook) twice.

## FOUNDATION HALF DOUBLE CROCHET *(abbreviated Fhdc)*

YO, insert hook in ch at base of Fhdc just made ***(Fig. 1)***, YO and pull up a loop, YO and draw through one loop on hook **(ch made)**, YO and draw through all 3 loops on hook **(Fhdc made)**.

**Fig. 1**

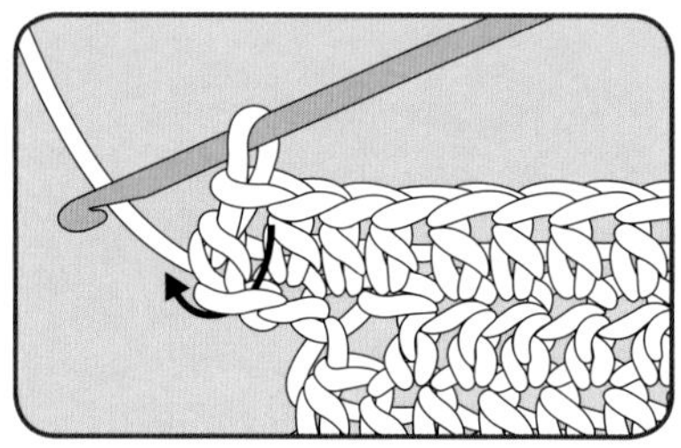

## FOUNDATION DOUBLE CROCHET *(abbreviated Fdc)*

YO, insert hook in ch at base of Fdc just made ***(Fig. 2)***, YO and pull up a loop, YO and draw through one loop on hook **(ch made)**, (YO and draw through 2 loops on hook) twice **(Fdc made)**.

**Fig. 2**

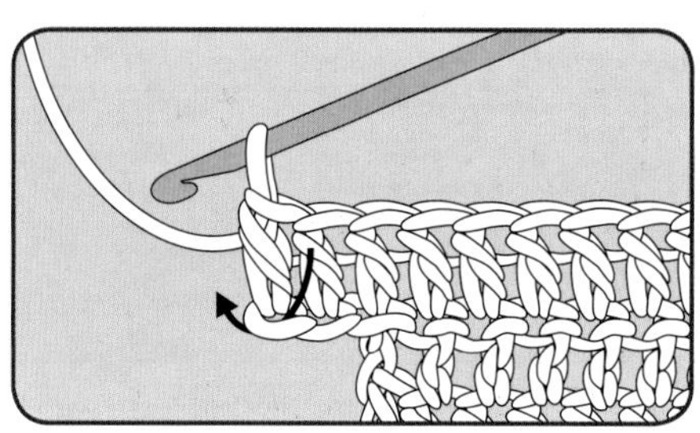

## BACK RIDGE OF A CHAIN

Work only in loops indicated by arrows ***(Fig. 3)***.

**Fig. 3**

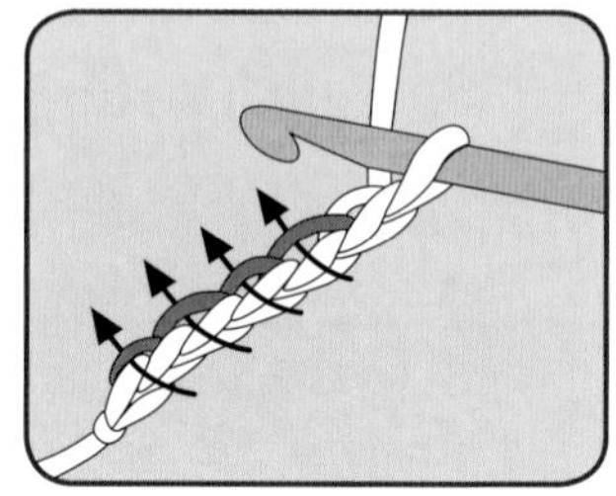

## BACK OR FRONT LOOPS ONLY

Work only in loop(s) indicated by arrow ***(Fig. 4)***.

**Fig. 4**

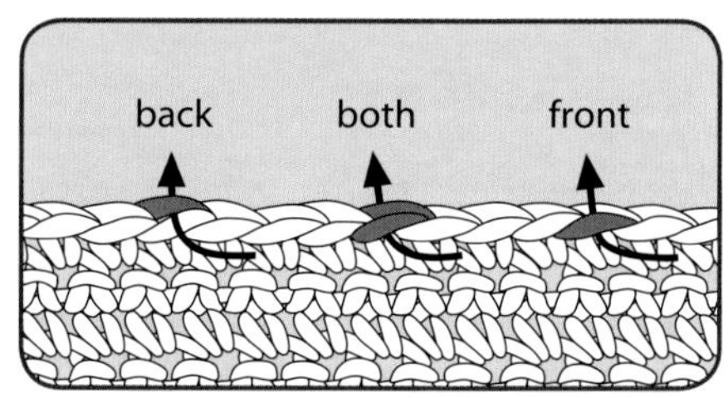

## FREE LOOPS

After working in Back or Front Loops Only on a row or round, there will be a ridge of unused loops. These are called the free loops. Later, when instructed to work in the free loops of the same row or round, work in these loops ***(Fig. 5a)***.

**Fig. 5a**

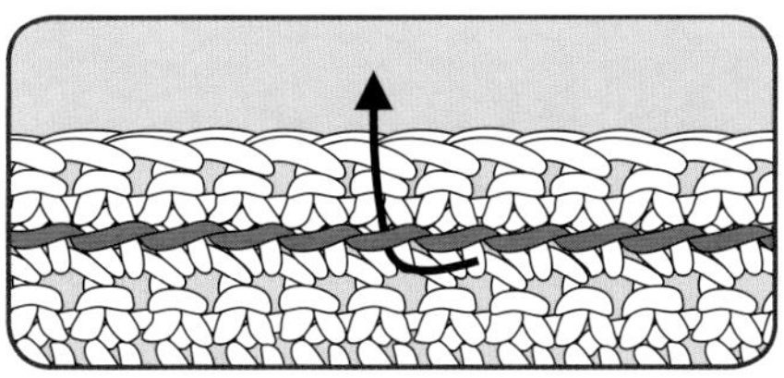

When instructed to work in free loops of a chain, work in loop indicated by arrow ***(Fig. 5b)***.

**Fig. 5b**

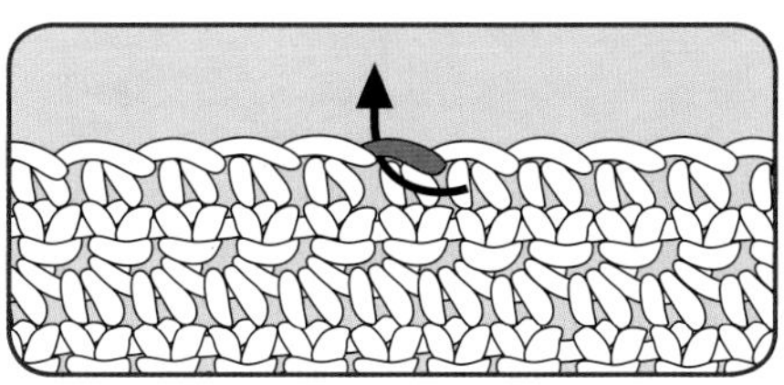

## WORKING BEHIND A STITCH

Work in stitch indicated, inserting hook in direction of arrow ***(Fig. 6)***.

**Fig. 6**

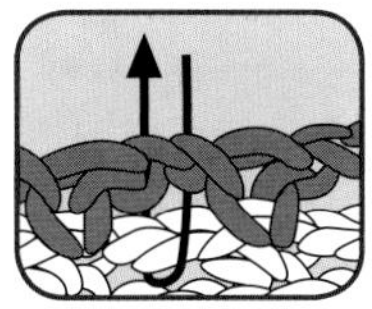

## WHIPSTITCH

With **wrong** sides together, sew through both pieces once to secure the beginning of the seam, leaving an ample yarn end to weave in later. Insert the needle from **back** to **front** through **both** loops on **both** pieces ***(Fig. 7)***. Bring the needle around and insert it from **back** to **front** through the next loops of both pieces. Continue in this manner across, keeping the sewing yarn fairly loose.

**Fig. 7**

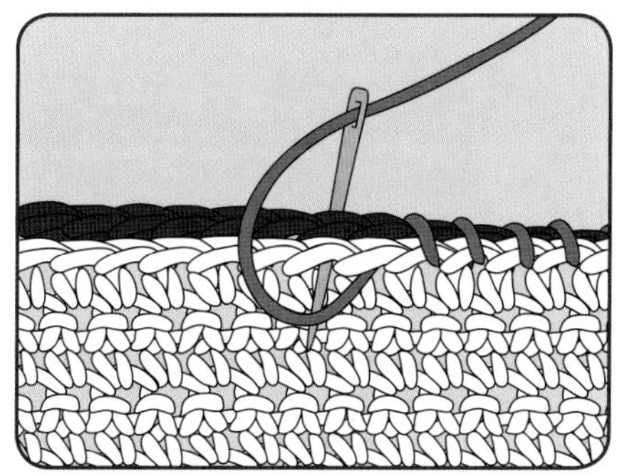

| Yarn Weight Symbol & Names | LACE 0 | SUPER FINE 1 | FINE 2 | LIGHT 3 | MEDIUM 4 | BULKY 5 | SUPER BULKY 6 | JUMBO 7 |
|---|---|---|---|---|---|---|---|---|
| Type of Yarns in Category | Fingering, size 10 crochet thread | Sock, Fingering, Baby | Sport, Baby | DK, Light Worsted | Worsted, Afghan, Aran | Chunky, Craft, Rug | Super Bulky, Roving | Jumbo, Roving |
| Crochet Gauge* Ranges in Single Crochet to 4" (10 cm) | 32-42 sts** | 21-32 sts | 16-20 sts | 12-17 sts | 11-14 sts | 8-11 sts | 6-9 sts | 5 sts and fewer |
| Advised Hook Size Range | Steel*** 6 to 8, Regular hook B-1 | B-1 to E-4 | E-4 to 7 | 7 to I-9 | I-9 to K-10½ | K-10½ to M/N-13 | M/N-13 to Q | Q and larger |

*GUIDELINES ONLY: The chart above reflects the most commonly used gauges and hook sizes for specific yarn categories.

** Lace weight yarns are usually crocheted with larger hooks to create lacy openwork patterns. Accordingly, a gauge range is difficult to determine. Always follow the gauge stated in your pattern.

*** Steel crochet hooks are sized differently from regular hooks–the higher the number, the smaller the hook, which is the reverse of regular hook sizing.

# YARN INFORMATION

The Dresses in this book were made using Light Weight Yarn. Any brand of Light Weight Yarn may be used. It is best to refer to the yardage/meters when determining how many balls or skeins to purchase. Remember, to arrive at the finished size, it is the GAUGE/TENSION that is important, not the brand of yarn.

For your convenience, listed below are the specific yarns used to create our photography models. Because yarn manufacturers make frequent changes in their product lines, you may sometimes find it necessary to use a substitute yarn or to search for the discontinued product at alternate suppliers (locally or online).

### JASMINE

***Caron® Simply Soft® Light™***
#0003 Honey

### LEXXI

***Patons® Grace™***
Black - #62040 Night
White - #62005 Snow
Red - #62705 Cardinal

### ASHLEY

***Bernat® Softee® Baby™***
Tan - #30010 Little Mouse
Peach - #30410 Soft Peach
Variegated - #30011
Little Mouse Marl
Rose - #30424 Soft Red
White - #02000 White

### KATE

***Bernat® Softee® Baby™***
Aqua - #30201 Aqua
***Lion Brand® Ice Cream***
Variegated - #306 Rainbow

We have made every effort to ensure that these instructions are accurate and complete. We cannot, however, be responsible for human error, typographical mistakes, or variations in individual work.

Instructions tested and photo models made by Debra Garcia, Raymelle Greening, and Barbara Schou.

Production Team: Instructional/Technical Writer - Lois J. Long; Editorial Writer - Susan Frantz Wiles; Senior Graphic Artist - Lora Puls; Graphic Artist - Kytanna McFarlin; Photo Stylist - Lori Wenger; and Photographer - Jason Masters.